A Snowflake in My Hand

A Snowflake in My Hand

SAMANTHA MOONEY

DELACORTE PRESS / ELEANOR FRIEDE

Published by
Delacorte Press/Eleanor Friede
1 Dag Hammarskjold Plaza
New York, N.Y. 10017

Manufactured in the United States of America

First printing

Designed by Judith Neuman

Library of Congress Cataloging in Publication Data
Mooney, Samantha.
  A snowflake in my hand.

  1. Cats—Anecdotes. 2. Mooney, Samantha.
3. Veterinarians—United States—Biography. I. Title.
SF445.5.M67 1983   636.8'089'0924 [B]   82-18328
ISBN 0-440-07935-7

To Mom and Dad—
for memories
and for dreams

I would like to thank Nick Lyons, who guided and encouraged me at every step. His support was unfaltering from the beginning.

I thank Eleanor Friede, Barbara Bowen, and Jeanne Bernkopf for their special care, attention, and expertise. . . .

I extend my gratitude to the clients and patients at our clinic who have allowed me to share a few moments in their lives.

My footsteps mount the slight incline, the first
to pass this way. The snow falls gently, muffling
New York City's shrieking sounds. My mind,
unfocused, follows up the hill and on to Maine.
Wooded, solitary chambers of silence broken only
by the crunching of snow packed underfoot.

Then I see him, and he summons all my senses
and awakens me, as he always does, to the reality
about him. The black cat poses on the windowsill,
grooming his glossy coat as if to punctuate his
contrast with the snow. The domesticated panther,
he sits in his jungle of houseplants and shares the
sun with them. But it is his ledge, and he has inched
the plants precariously edgeward to accommodate
his lengthy well-being. I smile to think of the plants
that have been swept off the carpet and repotted,
and wonder if the new window display is his.

I do not know his people, but in the years that I
have marked my progress by his presence in the
window, I have felt a fondness for those who love
him. Strangers they remain, these folk who feed
and fawn over their sassy cat, but I have singled out
their brownstone, this brownstone, mirrored by
brownstones. This is where the black cat lives.

Chapter 1

My alarm clock failed to ring, but by skipping morning coffee I managed to be only fifteen minutes late. As the elevator crawled to the eighth floor of the Animal Medical Center I hoped that perhaps Clancy too had overslept. It was 7:20. The elevator door opened, and I stepped into the hall to find him waiting.

"I know I'm late, Clancy, but it happens occasionally." He looked angry. "If you would just wait until I come get you, you wouldn't have to pace in the corridor."

I unlocked the office door, and he brushed past me as he entered. I opened the drawer immediately, knowing there would be no peace until he got what he wanted. Clancy was not a finicky eater and promptly concentrated on his breakfast.

He was a square-jawed, tiger-suited cat, seven years old.

Short-legged and sturdy, he looked like a prize fighter who had retired from the ring.

When I was on time, I would find him in his cage in the ward if the wardman had remembered to close the cage door securely. The door had to be lifted slightly for the lock to click. As soon as I opened the cage Clancy would meow, hug me, and then crawl over my shoulder and jump to the floor. Before I did the morning treatments, I would open the ward door so that he could run to the office where the food was waiting. But if I was even five minutes late, he would meet me at the elevator, as he had today, and reprimand me. I never knew how he got out the ward door.

Dr. Hayes came into the office. Audrey had completed her residency at the Animal Medical Center with a specialty in oncology, the study of masses or tumors. She was now an associate staff member. We had first worked together on Saturday night medical clinics. We both liked working with cats, and we both were unconventional in our restraint techniques: we tried to pay attention to the cat's preferences.

Dr. Hayes patted Clancy on the head. He glared at her.

"You know, Samantha, Clancy's using you. He's a male chauvinist, just like T.C." T.C. was one of her six cats.

"That may be true, Audrey, but Clancy and I have an understanding." Clancy yawned and walked away, confident that I would defend him.

"He's rude, arrogant, and ungrateful."

"He's handsome and Irish."

I heard Greg's voice in the corridor outside the office. Dr. MacEwen was the head of the unit.

"In the parking lot? It must have come from the stables across the street. Will it be all right in this box? What about food?"

"I put some water in there and some bread," the clinic aide replied. "I'm just afraid to leave it downstairs in the clinic, in case someone knocks it over. It's quieter up here, if you don't mind, and I'll take it home this afternoon."

"Morning, Audrey, Sam." Greg was carrying a shoe box with tiny holes punched in the top. "One of the aides found this mouse, and I told her we'd keep it out of the way for her this morning. What's Clancy doing out?" We all turned and looked at Clancy now sleeping soundly on the counter, snuggled in a corner. I thought I saw his ear twitch, but he did not move.

"He's exhausted, Greg."

"He never does anything. Put him back in his cage."

"But he's sick."

"He's not sick. Granted, he has the feline leukemia virus, but it doesn't faze him in the least."

"But he was abandoned. He thinks no one loves him."

Greg was weakening, as he always did with Clancy. Looking at the shoe box, he said, "What about the—"

"Clancy's too tired even to notice. You know he can't sleep when he's in his cage."

"Poor Clancy," Greg replied, smiling as he left the office.

Clancy stretched and shifted his position.

I had first met Clancy a few months after I started working in Oncology. We see most of our cancer patients on the eighth floor, but I was still working Tuesday and Saturday nights with Greg and Audrey in the general clinic on the second floor, where medical and surgical cases, routine examinations, vaccinations, and emergencies are handled.

When I walked into the exam booth that Tuesday night, Clancy was sitting on the metal table. I usually have to pry my cats out of their carrier when they visit the doctor, so I was impressed by his nonchalance. He stared at me defiantly and then began to groom himself. When Greg came in, Clancy lay on his side and stared wistfully into space.

Clancy's owner had three cats. The other two had tested negative for the feline leukemia virus. Because the virus is contagious among cats, Clancy's mistress had brought Clancy to be euthanized. He was her husband's cat; she had brought him in because her husband could not bear to.

Leukemia is an abnormal proliferation of white blood cells in the bloodstream and bone marrow. In cats most leukemias are caused by the leukemia virus, but not all cats with the virus develop leukemia.

The virus, found in a small percentage of cats in the general population, can be passed from cat to cat in the saliva, urine, milk, and blood. In other words, a communal litter pan and feeding dishes are likely intermediaries for the virus, as are a bite wound, or a mother cat nursing her kittens. Not all cats exposed to the virus will become viremic, or persistently infected. Some cats develop antibodies against the virus within three months of exposure to a positive cat, and therefore become immune to the infection.

We had been able to send a magnificent long-haired cat home to his grateful owner after the cat rejected the leukemia virus on his own. We didn't see a case like this often, but such things did happen.

We do not know which cats will become viremic and which immune, but we believe that kittens and older or debilitated cats are more susceptible because their immune systems are either not fully developed or are altered. In any event it takes more than one test to confirm that a cat has the virus.

A cat who tests positive for the leukemia virus may be a healthy pet with a glossy coat, good appetite, and normal activity. I remember a feisty calico cat with eyes the colors of stained glass who probably became positive late in her life. She lived to the age of twenty-one.

I had long been fascinated by this virus that remains dormant in some cats and causes fatal diseases in others. It was generally believed that the positive cats were more susceptible to disease because their immune systems, the body's defense, were suppressed by the leukemia virus. I had asked Greg if we could use on Clancy a new form of therapy that we had been testing—therapy meant to stimulate Clancy's immune system so that, ideally, he would reject the virus, or at least resist the diseases associated with the virus. Greg had agreed, and we had suggested this treatment to Clancy's mistress as an alternative to euthanasia.

When I lifted Clancy from the table, he had rested both front paws on either side of my neck. As we headed for the elevator to take us to the eighth floor, his new home, I heard Greg's voice. "Just this one, Sam. And remember, don't get too attached." But Clancy was purring.

Greg set the ground rules for Clancy's stay with us. Clancy must remain in a cage. He must not interfere with the Oncology Unit's routine. I appealed to Greg's sense of fairness. After all, Clancy was a pet, unaccustomed to prolonged confinement. Greg gave Clancy his first inch, and Clancy slowly and relentlessly stretched it until the entire eighth floor was his.

Clancy was allowed in the office before clinic for breakfast. Duerrel, our wardman, usually cleaned the ward between 7 and 9 A.M., and then Clancy could return to a clean cage. A few mornings clinic started early, and by the time his cage was ready I was busy with patients. Clancy wisely camouflaged himself among plants and piles of records. He slept soundly in the sun, only occasionally rattling a paper or toppling a plant as he shifted positions.

Greg was off on Saturdays, and Clancy spent that entire day in the office. He was so well behaved that gradually he came to stay with us a few days during the week. To encourage him to remain in his corner during clinic I left a water bowl, canned food and dry food within easy reach. But all too often when Greg was concentrating on a patient's X ray, Clancy, a noisy eater, would interrupt with a crunch or slurp.

Still, as time went on Clancy was allowed five-day access to the office, although Greg never actually acknowledged the concession.

Some afternoons Clancy would sit in Greg's office across the hall. While Greg worked at his desk Clancy slept curled up on the extra chair. But as soon as Greg left the office for a few minutes Clancy jumped down, stretched, and then took possession of Greg's chair, which he clearly preferred. When Greg returned, he always displaced Clancy from the chair, but he never threw him out of the office. And sometimes I would catch Greg reaching over and gently petting the slumbering beast.

The song that Clancy purred to me the first night he entered my life became a vital part of my days for the next two years. His former owners never called or came to visit Clancy. I guess they thought that any contact with him would be too painful for them. He was my cat now, and we spent our days learning about one another. Those days were precious days, bonus days for Clancy and me.

I learned one thing quickly about Clancy: he could not be trusted. I had completed morning treatments in time for clinic, despite my late start that morning. Greg walked back into the office and glanced at Clancy.

"Samantha, your cat's into something, again."

I reached over to extract the string or other inedible that he always finds, just as my eyes fell on the overturned shoe box. My fingers had already grasped the slimy object in his mouth when I realized that it was the partially devoured tail and hindquarters of Greg's mouse. "Clancy, that's terrible."

But Clancy disagreed. He strode boldly to his sunny den, stretched his stocky legs, and concentrated on cleaning his right front paw.

Chapter 2

Oncology has daily clinics on the eighth floor. I work with a team of three doctors, treating animals who have cancer. As research associate with the unit, I work in clinic, treat our hospital patients, and participate in any special projects or studies involving cats. I maintain records for the unit and assist in compiling data, writing, and editing publications.

The clinic was always busy, and I learned by listening to the doctors and by watching their examinations what questions were pertinent. Some of the doctors were especially patient in answering my questions when I first began working. They explained the tests that they ran, the diagnoses they made, and the treatments they prescribed. Most of our animals are seen on an out-patient basis. We see as many as 125 patients a week, and 75 percent are rechecks or scheduled treatment visits.

The waiting room decor is limited to a few plants. The room itself needs painting, but the painting must wait until the ceiling tiles are replaced, and these will only be replaced when the air-conditioning and heating units are repaired. Still, there is a lovely view of the Fifty-ninth Street Bridge and the East River. We can see the helicopters land across the street.

We have three examination booths which open onto the waiting room. They are separated by partitions that begin six inches from the floor and extend only partway to the ceiling.

Each day has basically the same beginning, but each day holds the promise of a few new faces, a hundred possibilities, and perhaps one miracle.

Monica Cosgrove was sitting with Mykonos when I walked into the waiting room.

"Which is heavier," I asked, "Mykonos or his record?"

"His record is heavier than he was when we first came here, but now I think he's got it beat!"

Mykonos was a large white Persian who had been coming in periodically for two years for treatment. He was sent to us originally as a possible cancer patient. Monica had taken him to several doctors when he began to have diarrhea. She had changed doctors and treatments in desperation as he continued to lose weight. She had watched helplessly as he grew weaker, and she had gained no support from friends who advised her to euthanize the poor cat. She could not end his life without knowing for certain that she could not help him. Finally one of the doctors in our general clinic on the second floor examined him and discovered thickened intestinal loops

11

and an enlarged abdominal lymph node. He performed some tests that indicated that Mykonos might have cancer, and referred him to Oncology. We repeated the tests and found that Mykonos had a higher than normal number of white blood cells in his peripheral blood and bone marrow. An abnormal percentage of these cells were eosinophils.

Eosinophils are white blood cells produced in response to allergies, parasite infestation or any foreign stimulation. We biopsied the thickened part of Mykonos's intestine and the enlarged abdominal lymph node, removing a small piece of tissue for examination. The results indicated that his intestines were inflamed, but we didn't know why.

Mykonos did not have cancer. What he needed was treatment to stop the abnormal production of eosinophils that was aggravating his condition. We treated him with chemotherapy, and within five months his abdomen was normal and so were his blood tests.

Mykonos was sprawled on the table while Audrey finished examining him.

"No diarrhea?" she asked.

"He had a little last night," Monica replied. Because of her conscientiousness we knew that we could try to lengthen the intervals between treatments without endangering Mykonos's health. Monica was aware of the subtle shifts in his mood, and she could tell when he was depressed.

"Well, we'll go ahead and treat him, then. I think we'll try to go five weeks again, if his blood test is normal."

"Yes, that seems to be the longest possible interval right now," she agreed.

We took the blood sample from his hind leg. The blood test would show us whether he had an increased percentage of eosinophils and an elevated white blood cell count; if so, he would need more frequent treatments. I held on to his leg to make sure that he wasn't bleeding once the needle was removed. He didn't mind the bloodletting procedure as much as the protective measures that followed.

"Hold on, sir," I requested as he attempted to pull his leg away. "I'll give it back to you, although I must admit, I like this foot very much."

As the Cosgroves left, Greg was seeing Tabby Rodolitz in another booth. She was an eighteen-year-old calico cat. Tabby had a recurrent fibrosarcoma on her left front leg. A fibrosarcoma is a malignant growth that develops in fibrous connective tissue. Tabby had undergone surgery twice in two months because the tumor had grown back. The veterinarian who sent her to us felt that he could not completely excise the mass now. The tumor was growing around the tendons and extended as far as the bone. We had tried immunotherapy injections for three months, but the mass continued to grow. As I walked into the room Greg was examining Tabby's leg.

"Mrs. Rodolitz, I think our options are exhausted at this point. The immunotherapy doesn't seem to be working at all, and the mass is too extensive for surgery."

"Why can't we amputate the leg?" asked Mrs. Rodolitz.

"Tabby's eighteen years old, and it's questionable whether she could tolerate the surgery. I really couldn't recommend an amputation on a cat this age."

"But she's healthy otherwise, and she doesn't even use the leg now, so she wouldn't really miss it. I can't put her to sleep, Dr. MacEwen, not without giving her every chance."

I was petting Tabby as they were talking, and smiled as she raised her hindquarters each time I stroked her. She was purring loudly.

"She does seem to be in good shape," Dr. MacEwen conceded. "Let's run some blood tests and X rays, and then go from there."

Greg and I went into the office to fill out the radiology request for Tabby.

"What would you do if she were your own cat?" he asked.

"Before I came here, I'm not sure," I replied. "But now I'd have to give her this chance."

Mrs. Rodolitz was an unusual client. Most of our clients feel an immediate aversion to the idea of amputation, believing that the result will be painful for their pets. Since we often understand our cats in terms of our own feelings, it is natural that the idea of amputation creates an image of handicap and readjustment to an altered life-style. But cats are graceful, adaptable animals. They can function normally with three legs, still able to outrun two-legged creatures when they choose. While it is true that a patient may be sore for a few days after surgery, the discomfort is slight compared to the suffering when the tumor is still present and growing. Besides, most of the patients are no longer using the involved leg by the time that we consider surgery.

The owner will not be present to share with us the moment of that first ventured step, or the first meal after surgery. Ambulatory, free from pain, and hungry, the cat is ready to go home. The owner will have the joy of seeing her cat thrive at home. The pain and discomfort are over; the cat makes the adjustment easily. There are no emotional crises to face. Cats don't worry about what other cats will think. They are remarkable survivors.

One owner told me she cringed when her three-legged cat first jumped out of the carrier. She described watching him fall the first time he attempted to reach the counter. Instinctively I touched her arm to hold her back. "Yes," she smiled, "he had to work it out himself. On the second try he made it."

"If she were mine," I told Greg again, "yes, I'd have to try."

Tabby's X rays and blood tests confirmed her health, and she was scheduled for surgery the next day. Our surgeon, Jay Harvey, planned to operate on her early in the morning. She could recover from the anesthesia and from the procedure itself during the rest of the day and, we hoped, go home the following day. I brought her into the ward and found a sunny cage for her.

I thought Jay was one of the finest surgeons at the center. He had trained at the center and then moved to California for a one-year residency program. When he returned, he was interested in specializing in surgical oncology. It was important for the Oncology Unit to work with a surgeon who was aware of the special problems involved in many of our cases. Most of our patients were older dogs and cats. Some of them were being treated for other problems as well, such as diabetes or heart disease, and therefore were considered greater surgical risks. Some of the surgery might cause disfigurement, especially if it involved tumors on the face and in the mouth. Jay had achieved a remarkable balance in his approach to surgery. He would perform an extensive procedure, always remembering that his patient was a pet whose postoperative life must be as normal as possible. He would operate to relieve pain or discomfort even if he could not cure. When he advised against surgery, it was because he believed that he could not help the animal and did not want to subject the pet to an unnecessary operation. He was fast and thorough. More than this, however, he was constantly aware of the patient under the surgical drape. His sense of responsibility didn't end with the operation, and many times we would meet in the recovery room where we both went to check on a patient. We met again at Tabby's cage when she was recovering from anesthesia. Jay had put her under a heat lamp because she was cold after the surgery.

"I think we'll leave her in Intensive Care overnight, just so she'll be watched," he said.

"She's waking up already," I commented as she began moving her hind legs and moaning softly.

"You know we repeated the X rays on her." He smiled. "We couldn't believe the chest films were those of an eighteen-year-old cat. We thought maybe Radiology had mixed up their patients!"

Three hours after surgery Tabby was recovering in Intensive Care. Everyone fussed over her, and through the crowd I saw that she was eating baby food. She went home the next day.

Mrs. Rodolitz waited on the second floor while I brought Tabby out in her carrier. She opened the box, and Tabby trilled to her.

"She's relieved to have that awful mass gone, I think," she commented. Mrs. Rodolitz didn't even seem to notice the shaved fur and the suture line that closed the layers of skin where Tabby's leg had been. She was so happy that Tabby was alive and comfortable that she didn't even ask how soon the fur would grow back.

Tabby continued to climb trees and rule her household for two years. We saw her for periodic rechecks and vaccinations. Tabby's extra years were playful and adventurous, and we were all proud to have been a part of her twenty-year life. Every time that Greg recommended amputation for a cat, he remembered Tabby.

Chapter 3

Toward the end of a busy morning clinic Clancy sat up and yawned. Lately I had noticed that while we worked in clinic, as Clancy grew more confident, Clancy worked on Greg. When the waiting room was full and people were standing out in the hallway, Greg frequently became tense. The change was visible in his face: no smiles, no extraneous comments. Clancy seemed to sense the change even before I did. Stretching his sleepy tiger body, he would stroll down the counter to the spot where Greg was leaning, writing in a record. Clancy would deliberately walk across the record to sit on the other side, with his tail still draped across it. Greg moved the tail. Clancy flicked it back. Greg moved the record. Clancy shifted his position. Greg put down the pen and considered throwing Clancy on the floor. Clancy whipped the pen off the counter with his tail and sauntered back to the window. The tension was broken, and Greg almost always smiled. If Clancy was wrong, he ended up back in his cage, but I guess he felt it was worth the gamble.

I was in the ward that afternoon when Greg walked in. The ward houses twenty-eight medium-size stainless steel cages, twelve smaller cages, and a large run. One bank of fourteen cages and the run overlook the river. In the morning the sun enters every cage on one side of the ward, and I always try to admit animals to that side.

"Sam, I need a cage for a cat I examined last night," Greg said. Some of the doctors worked in private practice on their evenings off from the Animal Medical Center. "He's going to stay with us for a while. He has a bloody pleural effusion and is very easily stressed," he explained. A pleural effusion is the accumulation of fluid in the chest cavity. The pressure from the fluid can compress the lungs and cause the animal breathing difficulty.

"Why don't his owners want to keep him?" I asked, for they were donating the cat to us.

"They have thirty-some dogs and cats already, and they really can't afford to pursue a diagnosis, especially when it doesn't look very promising. He's been losing weight, and he's not even eating now. They wanted to give him a chance, but they can't keep him."

It was not unusual for our Animal Medical Center clients to have more dogs and cats than they might have originally set as their limit. The people who care enough to ensure the well-being of their pets also frequently can't ignore a stray or injured pet. Apartment living generally restricts the number, however. In our new patient's case food and shelter were not enough. Moreover, it was possible that his illness was contagious and might endanger the health of the other cats. A large number of animals in a limited space is an unhealthy, stressful situation for the animals and their would-be protectors.

Siggie arrived in a cardboard pet carrier that said "I'm going home." Greg was opening the carrier and I saw the tiger stripes. "Oh, he's so"—at this point the cat looked up at me—"long," I finished. Perhaps because of his thinness his length seemed exaggerated. His Roman nose only added to the impression. He was trembling. He looked worried and intense beyond his three years. As I put him in his cage he seemed to disappear against the wall.

Greg suspected that Siggie had a mass in his chest that was pressing against the esophagus to cause gagging and vomiting. Siggie's history, age, and symptoms were suggestive of lymphosarcoma, a malignant tumor involving the lymph glands. We submitted blood samples and the fluid that we had removed from his chest. Radiographs confirmed the presence of a mass above his heart. Then we waited for the results.

The tests revealed that Siggie did not have feline leukemia or lymphosarcoma. We still didn't know what he did have. He continued to lose weight and to sit trembling in his cage. When he did eat, he vomited. I walked in as Greg and Audrey were reviewing Siggie's record a week after he had arrived.

"Greg, I think we have to consider surgery before he gets too weak. We can't treat him without a diagnosis, and he can't go much longer without treatment."

"I think you're right, Audrey, but we also have to consider expenses at this point. A thoracotomy is a major procedure, and we can't be sure that his disease is treatable even with a diagnosis."

An exploratory thoracotomy would involve opening Siggie's chest to determine what was causing his problems. If the surgeons felt that they could remove the mass, which we were hoping was the thymus, then the procedure would become a thymectomy. If the mass was more diffuse and involved lymph nodes or was in itself too extensive to remove, then they would biopsy it, removing what they could, close him up, and await the pathology results.

"Who's going to pay for this?" Greg continued. "The unit has paid the bill so far, but we have to be realistic. The cat doesn't belong to anyone. We may have to get our diagnosis at postmortem."

But for seven days I had fed and cared for this trembling, pathetic Siggie cat. I had grown fond of him, and he was responding to my attention. Holding the striped bundle in my arms, I turned to them.

"Listen," I began, "I have this cat who needs a thoracotomy."

They smiled, looking relieved.

"We'll get Jay to do it tomorrow."

Jay was not scheduled for surgery the next day, but he spoke to Dr. Steve Withrow, a second-year surgical resident. Steve was interested in oncology cases and worked closely with the unit. It was a two-man procedure, and he and Jay arranged their schedules to accommodate Siggie and his new owner.

I asked Jay to let me help anesthetize Siggie, because he was such a nervous patient. The surgical area was new to him, and I thought that he might feel more secure if he knew I was there. Jay asked if I wanted to stay during the procedure, and I accepted. I was nervous and silent as I sat and watched the machine that recorded Siggie's heartbeat. Finally I heard Steve's voice. "It looks good, Sam. I think I can get the whole thing." I knew he was smiling through his surgical mask. They removed the mass from Siggie's chest and submitted it for histologic diagnosis. Siggie went to Intensive Care, and while he recovered from the anesthesia I went home.

Living so close to the hospital enables me to stop by any evening to check on a patient. I love being able to do this. But it is being home that allows me time and space apart from my work. Time to think things out, to balance my life with other interests, to widen the channels of experience that, at the hospital, so often end in death. Here at home I am living with diversity. I am worker, student, daughter, friend. I am independently the head of a household. Home allows me the precious time to remember, to feel, and to dream. Home is the world that I share with my own four cats. I return every day to Natasha, Daphne, Frederick, and Sam. They delight me with their antics, discovering old toys and new tricks. Grooming one another or stretching between naps, they reassure me with their well-being. They comfort and strengthen me with their love.

Sometimes my cave, sometimes my castle, home is where they are. And soon Siggie would be a part of that refuge.

When I returned that night, Jay had already visited him and tried to feed him. Siggie waited, however, and when I came, he ate some baby food and purred for my benefit. The mass removed was a thymoma, a benign growth involving the thymus, and an extremely rare occurrence in cats.

After I brought Siggie home, I took a few days off from work to be with him. He no longer trembled and was eating voraciously. He adjusted well to my other cats, but then he had had a lot of practice in his other home. Siggie is now a sixteen-pound, glossy-coated tiger with a very long nose. He is eleven years old.

Natasha, Daphne, Frederick, and I moved to our present home a year after I began working at the center. The former tenant left me his cat, Sam, to care for temporarily while he got settled in California. But he never really got settled, and so Sam became a permanent member of our household. The two girls and he ignored each other, but Sam and Frederick immediately fought for dominant male status. They are equal in size, each weighing fifteen pounds. Frederick is gray and black tiger-striped with a spotted stomach, and Sam looks like a lumbering polar bear, all white with a few streaks of silver on his forehead. After all these years they have not stabilized the arrangements and periodically revive the controversy. Frederick was declawed by his former owner; my other cats are not. Some of the most difficult cats that we work with at the hospital are declawed. Their aggressive behavior is probably intended to mask the fact that they feel defenseless. I think that is why Frederick behaves as he does toward Sam.

When Siggie came home, he and Frederick recognized one another as brothers of the tiger-striped clan. Perhaps because of his diminished physique Siggie was not a threat to Sam. In fact, Siggie served as a buffer. At night Natasha slept by my right foot, Daphne at my neck, Frederick and Sam at my left foot with Siggie sandwiched between them.

On my second day home I wandered over to the center to visit Clancy. This was the first time that I had been away from him for more than a weekend, and I missed him. I also knew that Greg would not let him out when I wasn't there.

Greg made security checks to impede any escape attempts.

Clancy meowed when he saw me, but remained in the back of his cage. Even when I opened the door, he lay still. He had not eaten. I looked at his record and saw that he had a fever. Greg had noted his abnormal behavior. Clancy was sitting in a corner of his cage with his back to the door, meowing. I took him into the office, and he seemed content to sit with me while I talked to him. I fed him, and he ate.

The next day his temperature and appetite were normal. He ignored me. If he was ill, he had recovered quickly; if he disliked the interruption of his daily routine, it was now reinstated. I was learning that I was an integral factor in determining the quality of his days.

Quality became a meaningful word in my experience at the center. It was the word that best explained why I worked in the Cancer Therapy Unit. Quality was the factor that balanced significantly against death. Cancer therapy was not only a means of delaying death; it was an effort to ensure the quality of life. Ten minutes of therapy a week could enable a cat to breathe normally, to eat without vomiting, to walk using hind legs that had been paralyzed.

Quality meant dealing with the cat's illness one day a week and concentrating on the cat for the remaining six. It meant the smile on a client's face when the X rays were free of evidence of any spread of the disease. It meant expanding the intervals between treatments and, in some cases, stopping treatment completely.

My family and friends are sometimes confused by my involvement in my work. They accept the fact that I believe in what the unit is working for, but I don't think they really understand why. I tried to tell them about Tabby's surgery, but most of them stopped listening when I mentioned that she was eighteen. They thought her too old for such a procedure. When I spoke about Siggie before we knew what his fate would be, most of my friends were distressed that a sick cat had to face surgery. He was too young to endure such an ordeal.

Perhaps their reaction is intended as a warning against my obvious involvement. I try to tell them about our owners' commitment. Owners are even more involved in the care of their pets. They arrange their schedule for treatments, give medication at home, notice behavior changes, and love their pets. The owners entrust their animals' medical care to us. How can I not become involved when an owner is willing to make this commitment?

Cancer, unlike politics and religion, is not a topic of controversy. No one is for it. But cancer is not another word for death. Neither is it a single illness for which there is one cure. Instead it takes many forms, and each form responds differently to treatment. There are stories of failures and the painful decisions that love demands. But there are also stories of cats with cancer who gain weight, who play and groom themselves, eat plants, and go to the country on weekends. For as long as they are happy.

In many cases we give our clients an average survival time, which is merely an estimate to help the client understand the prognosis. But what excites and encourages me is the cat who goes into remission and gains weight, who never experiences adverse drug reactions, and who sails past our average survival time without a pause.

Our patients have remarkable dignity. We cannot help all of them live long lives, but we can help many of them live good lives. Each one deserves the expertise of our unit and, even more, individual attention and concern. I work with cancer patients because they deserve someone who wants to be there with them. I want them to feel as safe, as comfortable, and as respected as they can in a hospital situation.

Quality is not duration or endurance. It is a timeless, elusive commodity. It is a word that, more than defining life, we strive to make synonymous with life for every patient.

Chapter 4

When the first snow fell in December I opened the window to bring a handful of nature inside for my cats. Daphne, the classic mischievous feline, attempted to get out through the open window. As soon as her front paws touched the cold, wet fire escape she reconsidered.

I've been careful about screenless windows since Natasha disappeared years ago. A friend was staying at my old apartment while I was away for the weekend, and he promised to take care of Daphne and Natasha. When I returned, he was out. Daphne met me at the door, ran past me into the hall, and headed for the staircase. I called her, and she pranced into the apartment, delighted with herself. I looked for Natasha, surprised that she was not at the door. Seeing my open window by the fire escape, I didn't wait for my friend's return. My next-door neighbor was out, but I thought that Tasha had most likely walked across the fire escape into his open window. I called her name through the closed door but didn't hear a reply. I climbed the stairs, remembering that Daphne, each time she ran into the hall, ran for the stairs leading up. I knocked on doors, but most people were at work. Those who were home had not seen her. The door to the roof was open, and I walked out.

The tar was soft beneath my feet, hot from the sun. On the roof of the building attached to mine a woman was hanging up her laundry to dry.

"What are you looking for, dear?" she asked when she observed me searching the roof, calling for Natasha.

"My cat," I replied. "My cat's gone." I was frightened now and verging on tears.

"What does she look like?" she asked. "Is she white and orange and—"

"And black," I said, completing her description of my calico. "Where is she?"

"I found her in the hall of my building," she explained. "I couldn't pick her up. But when I opened my door she came in."

I was so relieved that I interrupted again. "Will you take me to her?"

"Well, she's not there. This morning my husband opened the door, and she ran out. He saw her run up the stairs to the roof again."

I returned to my building and found that my weekend guest had returned. He had spoken to the man next door, who confirmed my original surmise. Natasha had entered his apartment through the open window. He simply opened the front door and let her out into the hall.

I checked outside the building, reluctantly looking in the backyard in case she had fallen from the roof. Relieved at not finding her there, I returned to my apartment and waited for my neighbors to return.

I was furious at my friend. I never left my windows open wide, and I always closed them when I left the apartment. Before I worked at the center, I closed the windows primarily as a precautionary measure. My apartment faced the back and was accessible by the fire escape. When I started working at the center, I discovered a more important reason for being careful.

We call them high-rise cats. These are the cats who fall off window ledges or fire escapes when their owners assume that cats, being graceful creatures, will not lose their balance. A bird, a loud noise, a sudden movement can startle them, and in that moment of distraction they fall. Some of them recover, depending upon how far they fell, how they landed, and what broke their fall. Many of them die.

I was explaining this to my guilty friend when we heard a commotion in the hall. A lovely old Italian lady who didn't speak English lived diagonally across from me. Her door was open, and she was in the hall trying to summon help. We ran to assist her, and she pulled me into her apartment, over to a large carved wooden wardrobe. I heard Natasha meow. As soon as she heard my voice she came out.

I don't know what my Italian lady expected to find, but she smiled when she saw Natasha. I imagine that she had heard my frightened kitty move or perhaps had seen movement without realizing how domestic her intruder was. We all returned to our proper homes, and my friend found new lodgings elsewhere.

Daphne didn't like lectures and concentrated on washing the dirty snow from her immaculate paws.

On Christmas Eve we finished clinic and met in the office to share good wishes and a drink. Monica Cosgrove had sent us six bottles of French champagne, as she had every year since Mykonos became our patient. The card read, "Thank you for another year." We opened a bottle.

Clancy loved Christmas. He loved the presents, loved sampling the food and then the boxes it was packaged in. He always managed to fit, no matter what the size. But as the days had grown shorter this year he had seemed to be slowing down. He still demanded to be out with his public, but he was less conspicuous. We found nothing specifically wrong with him, yet he was changing.

"Clancy didn't eat today," I mentioned as I opened a can of Super Supper, his favorite.

"I left my lunch out on the counter the other day, and he didn't touch it." Jay had previously shared his lunch unintentionally with Clancy, who had torn open the tinfoil, dragged out the roast beef, and rolled the apple under Jay's desk.

I watched as Audrey picked him up and examined him. She glanced at Greg and laughed nervously, as she does when she is uncomfortable or upset. Greg confirmed her findings. Clancy's kidneys were enlarged and irregular. He was still leukemia test positive. He was seven. I knew that lymphosarcoma involving the kidneys was a likely diagnosis. Jay walked over and put his arm around me. "We'll take care of him, Sam, don't worry. We're a pretty good team, aren't we?" I smiled back at him. Audrey had her coat on, and Jay went to get his.

"Merry Christmas. See you Friday." Greg reached over and patted the tiger-striped head. "Good night, old man."

I took the quilted blanket that I had made for Clancy and placed it beside him in the corner. His name was embroidered in green against the brown-and-mint paisley pattern. I kissed him on the striped M on his forehead, and he pretended to be sound asleep.

"It's okay, Clancy, you don't have to con me tonight. Merry Christmas, angel." I turned out the lights and locked the door. No one complained that he was not in his cage.

Christmas Eve was my favorite day of the year. I had celebrated in various ways over the years, at parties, with friends, or at concerts. But no matter where I was or with whom, I always wanted to be home on Christmas Eve.

This year was ending, and I felt my carefree days with Clancy slipping away. On this special night of sorrow and joy, of quiet wonder and peace, I went home to Natasha and Daphne, Frederick, Siggie, and Sam. Home was where I needed to be.

Christmas Day Audrey came in to check our hospital cases and to take phone calls. Even on holidays the clients are able to speak to a doctor on all services. In Oncology the three doctors alternated holidays, and Christmas was Audrey's turn. When she arrived, I had already fed Clancy. He ate a jar of beef baby food, and I gave him a special treat of roast beef. Then Audrey and I distributed the catnip mice that we had bought to the cats in the ward. Clancy got a blue mouse, but I think that he would have preferred the real thing.

I went home and opened three cans of Turkey and Giblets for my family's Christmas dinner, thinking that this was a traditional choice for the occasion. Only Siggie was grateful. Natasha presented herself appropriately in a Bloomingdale's box under the tree while Daphne removed the ornaments from the lower branches. Frederick and Sam seemed to respect the holiday cease-fire. Siggie ate everyone's food.

Chapter 5

Christmas was over. On Friday routine was reinstated at the center, and we scheduled Clancy for his biopsy. I sat with him in the recovery room, and many of his admirers stopped by to visit him. Jay had biopsied his kidneys. Clancy had lymphosarcoma. He was not a stoic patient, but he reserved his complaints for an audience. Left alone, he dozed. I carried him back to the eighth floor to his cage, where he would receive intravenous fluid therapy. He was exhausted and showed no reluctance to remain in his cage. When I left for the day, he was sleeping in his litter pan, and his fluid bottle was set up outside the cage for his night's treatment. At two o'clock the next morning the phone rang in my apartment.

"Samantha? This is AnneMarie." She was a night treatment nurse. "Do you have Clancy with you?"

"No—he's missing? But he was hooked up to fluids."

"Well, the bottle is there, but the connection tube is broken. His cage door was open when I came up to check him."

"He's not in the ward? Maybe someone put him in another cage."

"No, I checked the ward, and I've been calling up and down the hall for him. I thought maybe you had him, or that you'd know his hiding places."

"But he had surgery today," I reasoned. "He couldn't go far. I'll be right over."

"Samantha, how could he get outside the ward with the door closed?"

"I don't know. I've never known." I smiled as I pictured him sleeping soundly in his cage. He had outfoxed me again.

As I walked down the hill to the hospital I tried to outline a plan. His favorite spot was the storage area down the hall, but it was locked at night. I always had thought it was his favorite place because of the hysteria he created whenever Harold, the supply manager, who was wary of cats, saw him in there.

I checked the ward again and the office. Calling his name, I walked down the hall. A distant meow drew me to the storage room. As I continued calling his name his cries became louder and more urgent. A flashlight shone on two round eyes, and familiarity gave form to the surrounding darkness. Clancy had climbed the ten-foot grating and was sitting on the top shelf of the storage wall, insisting that he could not come down. After all, he was sick.

I rescued my little soldier, and he purred while I yelled and cried. That morning Harold complained that someone had torn into two fifty-pound bags of dry food, from the bottom.

We waited a week after Clancy's surgery to allow healing of the biopsy site. On January 2 we began treatment. Clancy growled and hissed, fighting his weekly chemotherapy treatments. But five minutes of discomfort for all of us was worth the change in him once his treatments began. Within a week after his first treatment his kidneys became smaller and his appetite increased. He was playful and curious again.

The beginning of each new year was a time of reflection for me. After the excitement of Christmas I found myself thinking back instead of anticipating the future. Subdued, reflective, and perhaps a little melancholy.

I was at home taking my tree down, kneeling on the floor and packing the surviving ornaments in boxes when I felt two paws on the back of my neck. I spun around and Frederick reached up again, standing on his hind legs, and hugged me. He had taught me that this gesture meant "pick me up," and he purred his approval. Is that what he had done in his former home? I wondered how his previous owner could have given him up. This magnificent tiger was brought to the hospital to be euthanized because his owner's fiancée was allergic to cats. He was a healthy adult cat whose life was almost terminated because his owner had made a choice.

I wondered about the previous life-styles of my adopted adult cats. They seemed to adjust quickly to the new environment, but I wondered about their kittenhood and their previous daily routines.

When I moved to my present apartment, Natasha and Daphne stretched as though it was the first time in their lives that they had had enough room. All the cats loved the space in the new apartment. I don't know how large Siggie's former place was, but he now galloped the length of his home, usually around 1 A.M., three or four times a week. In the old two-room apartment Natasha used to bring items from my laundry bag up the steps to my loft bed. Now when I had company, she could drag underwear from the bathroom, through five rooms, and drop it at the foot of my guest.

Sometimes at work I watched Clancy in a new situation, amazed at his adaptability. One of the television stations filmed a segment in the waiting room for a news program. They arrived after clinic, and Greg had arranged a late appointment for a dog with mammary gland tumors. When Greg finished the examination, there was still time for another segment. Clancy was helping the camera crew, jumping on boxes and examining their equipment. I suggested making him a TV star. Greg thought that we could pretend to give Clancy his treatment. I placed the star on the exam table. Lights, camera, and action as Greg reached for Clancy's leg, needle in hand. Clancy knew that he had just been treated the day before. He showed the film crew what a terrible experience this was for a helpless kitty. We finally settled for an episode showing Greg listening to Clancy's heart. Greg's head was bowed as Clancy looked straight into the camera.

Clancy, the star, made full use of the eighth floor accommodations. It was difficult to believe that he had once stayed in a cage for most of the day. He might stop by to visit Greg or wander down the hall to torment Harold.

Once when I went down to retrieve Clancy, Harold said, almost accusingly, "I thought you said he was sick." In his own way I think Harold actually cared. Clancy, with his stubborn perseverance, had conquered another heart. Harold let him sit in empty boxes and climb the mountains that appeared with each delivery. Only when Clancy got underfoot or when he maneuvered toward the dry food bags did Harold summon my assistance.

The new year had offered Clancy and me a compromise. Our careless routine was disrupted and a new one introduced. We would endure weekly therapy, and the weekly reminder that our lives had been altered. It was a compromise, but we accepted the terms. As much as I resisted it, change had worked its way into my routine.

The new year brought with it new faces, new names, new stories. The clinic waiting room was a mixture of familiar and unfamiliar faces, and cats whose visits I would soon begin to anticipate.

Mr. and Mrs. Berkeley were visiting our clinic for the first time. Denton was a nine-year-old black cat who had undergone a mastectomy elsewhere nine months ago. Jay and I went in to meet Denton and her owners.

"Do we know what the original biopsy was?" Jay asked as he examined her.

"The doctor said it was malignant," Mr. Berkeley replied.

"Well, she has recurrence along her mammary glands, and it feels as though it might have spread to her axillary lymph nodes."

"We were afraid it might have spread."

"We can take her to surgery, But I don't know if—"

"No," Mrs. Berkeley interrupted. It was the first time she had spoken. "No more surgery."

"Well," Jay continued, "I don't know if we could remove all the tumor, and I think she might have some problems healing in that area."

I knew that Jay would not insist upon surgery. If he believed that he could best help Denton by surgical removal of her tumor, he would have explained the procedure and the effect of the surgery on Denton's prognosis so that the Berkeleys could think about it. The tumor was in a difficult location, however, and Jay was concerned that not only might he not be able to remove it all, but also that the surgery might help spread the disease.

"Why don't we start her on immunotherapy today?" he suggested. "A series of sixteen weekly injections. Maybe this boost of her immune system will help to keep these tumors under control."

"Will she get sick from the treatment?" Mrs. Berkeley asked.

"Most of our cats don't. They seem to tolerate the therapy well. Some of them run a fever. Some may be depressed for a few hours after or not feel like eating, but usually they're fine by that night or the next morning. We'll monitor her response and find the best dosage for her. I think that's the best plan that we can offer you. We don't recommend using chemotherapy in cats with mammary tumors, because our results haven't been encouraging."

"No, we don't want to give her chemotherapy."

Mrs. Berkeley's reaction was not uncommon in our clinic. When I began working in the unit, we were using chemotherapy primarily on dogs. I was afraid of these drugs that killed both normal and abnormal cells. I was apprehensive about possible toxic effects, even though the dogs tolerated therapy well. Cats are not little dogs, however, and medication often affects them differently.

The first cat we treated with chemotherapy had lymphosarcoma and was leukemia test positive. I remember standing and watching him after his treatment, waiting for something to happen. What happened within twenty-four hours was that his chest mass decreased in size and his appetite increased.

I am still apprehensive about chemotherapy, although I am aware of its effectiveness. I worry about the effects of long-term therapy, recognizing that this concern in itself is a sign of our progress in treating disease. Chemotherapy is rarely a cure for our patients, but in many cases it provides valuable time. In some cases it enables us to combine therapy modes, shrinking a tumor mass enough, for example, for us to consider surgery that was previously impossible.

Most of our clients had personally observed the effects of chemotherapy on a friend or had heard tragic stories about such treatment. In human medicine they use much higher doses, and that may be one reason that their results are much better than ours. They aim for a cure, while we try to control the disease. We can't subject the owner or the cat to a helpless situation. We try to maintain the quality of the cat's life. In Denton's case more aggressive therapy with either surgery or drugs would certainly cause immediate discomfort for her, and would probably not ensure her a longer or better life.

There are certain disease forms that don't respond to conventional therapy. New modes of therapy can offer hope when we have nothing else to give. Our clients are informed about the possible consequences of therapy and advised of all the alternatives available. If one form of treatment works well in most cases, the client should be informed of that. Our patients aren't experimental animals. They are pets, and we believe that we owe them and their owners the benefit of our experience. We have enough diseases that don't respond to conventional therapy. Many owners are willing to try something new on the chance that it might work. But the choice must be theirs. And the decision has to be based on all the available information.

"She's your cat, isn't she, Mrs. Berkeley?" I asked, smiling at Denton's dependence on her. The golden eyes had not looked away from her face.

"Yes, we've been through a lot together."

I never saw Mrs. Berkeley again. Her husband brought Denton in every week, and during those visits we learned the history of their close relationship. Denton and Mrs. Berkeley were both diagnosed as having malignant breast tumors in March of the previous year. Mrs. Berkeley received chemotherapy and spent a lot of time at home with Denton. The treatments made her terribly ill. When they both had recurrences, Mrs. Berkeley wanted therapy for Denton, but only if it had minimal side effects. For three months Denton did quite well on this treatment, and both the Berkeleys were encouraged.

On a Saturday morning in late April I walked into the waiting room and saw Mr. Berkeley sitting there.

"Are you all right?" I asked him. He looked so tired.

"It's my wife," he started. "They took her to the hospital Thursday. She was so weak, and the treatments—they weren't working anymore."

"They can care for her better in the hospital," I said, "and they can make her more comfortable."

"But I don't know what to do," he said, his voice trembling. "I don't think they can help her. And now Denton."

"Why, what's wrong with Denton?"

"She stopped eating on Thursday, and she's been hiding under my wife's bed. She sleeps there all day."

I lifted the lid of the carrier and gently stroked Denton's black coat. She had lost weight and was breathing heavily.

"Dr. Harvey will be in shortly," I told him. "We'll find out what's wrong with Denton."

When Jay arrived I had the radiology request ready, and

he examined Denton briefly before sending her down for films.

Denton had metastatic lesions and fluid in her lungs. This meant that the cancer cells responsible for the growth in her mammary glands and in the adjacent lymph nodes had now started to grow in her lungs. Mr. Berkeley asked us to euthanize her. He stopped at the door and looked for one last time at Denton.

"She was my wife's cat, you know. Such a comfort to her. I don't think I can tell her."

Mrs. Berkeley died in the hospital three days later.

Some of our regular clients asked about Mr. Berkeley and Denton. They came in on the same day and usually chatted while awaiting their appointments. Our clients who were considering therapy were often aided in making their decisions by seeing other cats who were receiving treatment.

Mr. Berkeley had met a cat with mammary gland cancer who, after five years of therapy, now only came in every six weeks. He had met another black cat who had been coming in for three years after the owner's original doctor had suggested euthanizing the cat. But he also met a man with a Siamese cat that was not responding to therapy. Mr. Berkeley was in the waiting room when we euthanized that wonderful little Siamese.

Most of the friendships formed in the waiting room during those weekly visits didn't continue outside the hospital, but for a short time every week our clients were surrounded by other people who were committed to their animals. Perhaps the boss didn't understand why this employee had to take the cat in once a week, but the person sitting next to him on the waiting-room bench did.

Chapter 6

In February a new educational program started at the center. Students from the University of Maine came to participate in a work-study semester at the hospital. They were studying to become veterinary assistants and technicians. Lectures were given by the AMC doctors, but most valuable was the daily experience that the students gained from working in various areas of the hospital. The first group consisted of eight young women, and they were housed in a small apartment on the eighth floor. The apartment was located at the opposite end of the hall from our ward, next to the supply area. They had three small bedrooms furnished with bunk beds, and a kitchen. Across the hall was a living room with a desk, a sofa, a few chairs, and a television.

Clancy welcomed that first group of students in February,

pleased to share his new living quarters with them. What a remembered joy it must have been for him to sleep on a bed once again. He shared his wondrous self with all the girls. I found him on a different bed each time I came in to reclaim him. I suppose I could have been jealous, but Clancy made everyone feel special. He always acknowledged me with a trill, throwing back his head as though shaking an invisible mane. Sometimes he wandered back to the office on his own. He still slept in his cage at night, but now he had TV privileges. One of the students usually returned him to the ward, but I was not surprised, knowing Clancy's tactics, to find that occasionally he spent the night with the girls.

Day after day I watched his stocky legs carry those familiar tiger stripes past Greg's office and on down the hall. From the office I could hear the welcome he received, almost a daily ovation just for being Clancy.

Clancy was not a performing cat in the traditional sense. He watched me roll balls across the floor, fetch them, and roll them again. He watched me bounce them off the wall. He watched me lose them under the cabinets.

I bought him a mouse collection. Clancy had catnip mice, mice on wheels, battery-operated mice. He had fuzzy mice and rubber mice. He had mice in paisley, stripes, and solid colors. But Clancy knew the real thing.

I gave him a jumping frog, a chicken that pecked along the floor. I bought him a rubber fish and put it in his water bowl. Clancy watched me play with all my new toys. But the fish was too much. He walked over to his bowl to quench his thirst after a morning nap in the glaring sun, only to find something floating in his water. He looked at me as though I had offered meat loaf to a vegetarian. With his two-syllable meow, the one he used for urgency, he reiterated his disapproval. Clancy left the room, and, ashamed, I reeled in the fish.

The one game that he would play with me was itsy-bitsy spider. As Clancy slept in the corner on the counter the five-legged spider of my right hand would begin creeping toward him, accompanied by an a capella solo. He watched as it drew closer. He watched, showing no sign of participation. Finally, when the spider was within reach and I was convinced of Clancy's boredom, he grabbed the five-legged monster with both front paws and sank his teeth into its fleshy center.

The weeks flew by as Clancy made room in his life for all his admirers. He managed to please each one, finding time in his busy daily schedule to single us out for a few special moments.

On a Wednesday in April I saw Mrs. Smith in our clinic waiting room.

"Why don't you bring Oliver Cromwell in and we'll take a look at him," Audrey said. Mrs. Smith picked up the carrier and brought it into the exam room. Oliver was a normal cat who was feline leukemia test positive. We examined him every two or three months because, like Clancy, he was more susceptible to disease. We hoped that these routine examinations would enable us to detect any subtle changes in his physical condition and his blood profile. These periodic checkups also removed some of the pressure from Mrs. Smith. She knew that Oliver was a high-risk candidate for lymphosarcoma, and we all felt better about watching him closely.

Oliver was an impressive cat. He was tiger-striped like Clancy, but he had white markings on his coat.

"How was his last blood test, Dr. Hayes?" Mrs. Smith

asked. We had checked a complete blood count, looking specifically at the numbers of red and white blood cells. Too few white blood cells will not allow the cat to fight infection; too many may indicate the presence of a severe infection or of leukemia.

"Well, his white blood cell count and differential were normal, and he's not anemic. He's still positive for the leukemia virus."

"Yes, I don't suppose that's going to change," she replied. "It's been a while now since he's been taking those pills, but he seems so healthy."

"He checks out just fine. I can't find anything wrong with him."

"No, he wouldn't get sick now. He's going to Maine next month."

"Why did you bring along Topaze? Any problems?"

"No, but he hasn't been in for a while, and he likes to keep Oliver company. We left the girls at home."

Mrs. Smith and her daughter had four cats. Jenny, Samantha, and Topaze were leukemia test negative. When the Smiths discovered that Oliver was positive, the family had been together for six years. The three other cats were still negative, and although the Smiths knew that there was no guarantee that they would remain negative, they couldn't part with any of them. We put them all on the same therapy as Clancy received and tested them periodically.

They all adored Oliver, for he was the oldest and the most worldly. Every summer the Smiths took them to their home in Belfast, Maine. For Oliver and Topaze, Maine was their natural home. The girls were city cats.

Like Mrs. Smith, many of our clients have more than one cat and so we get to meet the entire family. We see cats with diabetes, heart disease, and skin disorders, do yearly vaccinations, discuss diet, and sometimes just clean the ears of a patient's littermate.

"May I say hello to Clancy?" Mrs. Smith asked. "He's lost some weight, hasn't he?"

She had not been in since before Christmas, so I told her about Clancy's illness.

I also told her about Clancy's new nightly routine, developed since the Maine students' arrival in February. I returned him to his clean cage at the end of the day. He immediately spilled the water, turned over his litter pan, defecated, and then meowed pitifully. How could I leave him overnight in that pigpen? Of course, I opened the door and picked him up. He sprang from my shoulder, and the chase was on. Every night I would leave him, finally, in a clean, dry, neat cage. And every morning I discovered a cage full of shredded paper. I wondered if he was working with internal security or else preparing confetti for a parade.

"They're alike in many ways, aren't they?" I said, looking from Clancy to Oliver. "Both seemed destined to be women's cats, our protectors."

"Yes," she answered, "they have a certain stoic nature."

"Perhaps it comes with nobility."

She promised to send us a postcard from Maine.

Clancy's birthday was May 17. It would be our third celebration together. The first week in May he became anemic and developed a fever. I had seen enough cats in our clinic to know that Clancy had reached the final stage. We could treat his symptoms, and he might respond temporarily. Greg asked me only once, early in the week, if I wanted to euthanize Clancy. But I had to try to help him. We treated him with blood transfusions and antibiotics for five days. He did not respond.

The Maine students came to visit him and carried him back to their room for short visits as he grew weaker. The nursing staff asked about him, and Harold, noting Clancy's absence, also inquired. I saw each one's concern. I told them he was dying. I felt their pain and mine touch for a moment, merging in our helplessness, and then shatter into separate fragments of grief and loss. How many friends my little fighter had made. How many barriers he had climbed to reach so many hearts.

Greg walked into the office Friday afternoon as I was treating Clancy.

"Did he eat today?" he asked.

"No, he doesn't even want baby food. His temperature just won't come down. It was 104.6 this morning." The normal range for a cat is 100–102.5.

"His kidneys are still small," he said as he examined him. "But he's so pale again."

I sat with Clancy awhile in the office. The door was open, and I thought how far Clancy had come from his early days with us. We never left the door open in those days, because Clancy would disappear for hours. Now he no longer cared. He was uncomfortable, and our treatments had failed. I recalled his one earlier illness, and the promise that I had made him about the quality of his life. My tough Irish rogue had put up quite a battle since Christmas, but looking at him asleep in my arms, I saw how exhausted he was.

"Greg, I don't think Clancy's happy anymore. I think he wants to die."

The tears that I had held back over these past days could be held back no longer once the words were spoken.

46

To choose euthanasia was to take a chance. A chance of missing a miracle. We had saved Clancy's life once, and we had acted in good faith. We had promised him a life different from his former life, but a good one. We had given him days of curiosity and exploration, days of food and rest, and more food, and countless hours in the sun. And he had lived them fully. In return, to my days he had added laughter and joy, fear and occasional anger, and responsibility. He had added love and, now, sorrow. When he became ill, again we had tried to improve his days and to extend their number. We succeeded for a short time. To save his life now, without a miracle, was impossible. We could keep him alive for a short time longer, but we could not restore the quality of his former days. To keep him alive now was not acting in good faith. It was selfish.

Greg prepared the injection, and I carried Clancy in his quilted blanket, his Christmas blanket, into the examination booth. I held him and felt his heart beating against my arm. As long as it beats, I thought, he's still with me. And once it stops, I'll never see him again. Looking in his trusting eyes, I saw him pacing at the elevator, pouting in his cage. I saw him as he was when he was well and happy.

He did not cry or struggle when the needle entered his vein. He died quickly in my arms. Alone in the room I kissed the M on his striped head, and said good-bye.

Chapter 7

When I was growing up in Buffalo, most of my summers were spent working at a camp in Dunkirk, New York, on Lake Erie. My brother was a lifeguard there, and I worked in the kitchen. I was up at 6 A.M. to make hot cereal for two hundred campers. Since I have been living in New York, a longing for space and water has still accompanied the appearance of pussy willows and lilacs in the florist shops, but now I long for the ocean—now I seek the unpredictable moods, the conflict and passion of waves, and the limitless visage of the Atlantic. And late that May after Clancy's death I needed the wordless comfort that a moment of communion promised.

Jay had arranged his schedule so that beginning in May he had weekends off. Throughout the year Oncology had resident AMC doctors rotating through our service. They worked in clinic or with Jay in surgery, depending upon their area of interest, for a month or six weeks. In this way they were introduced to the special problems encountered in oncology, and this brief exposure enabled them to explore their own feelings about working with cancer patients. Dr. Steve Arnoczky was a surgical resident, and he worked Saturday clinics when Jay shifted to a Monday-through-Friday schedule. Steve was thin and over six feet tall. His full-length lab coat fell several inches short of his knees. He had already decided to specialize in orthopedic surgery and was not particularly interested in oncology, but the staff and clients loved working with him. He was always playing jokes on us or making the clients smile.

Steve often had his camera with him to photograph interesting cases for lectures and teaching purposes. In oncology the responses to therapy were sometimes dramatically documented in photographs. One day earlier in the year, when I saw him taking pictures, I had mentioned how much I wanted photographs of some of our ward cats. He came upstairs with me and spent an hour patiently posing each cat, including Clancy. Months had passed, and I had forgotten about our photo session.

A week after Clancy died, I finished working a busy Saturday clinic. I enjoy steady clinics, but this one was hectic. I was preparing medication for one patient, one was waiting to be treated, and a third needed fluids. We had two cats in Radiology who had to be retrieved and another waiting to go down. Everything was getting done, but there was little time for more than what was required. No pleasantries, no ear-rubs for the cats, and no purrs in return. I felt that if one person asked me to do one more thing I might scream. I was already screaming inwardly. Steve noticed my tension and very seri-

49

ously asked me to run down to the cafeteria to get coffee for him. Just as Clancy could always reach Greg at a crucial moment, Steve made me laugh at myself.

Steve never said anything about Clancy's death, but he helped me through those empty days when my sadness was buried in efficiency, and my sense of loss magnified by moments with our patients. When clinic was over, Steve handed me a package. He had remembered the photographs, and on the top was a beautiful picture of Clancy.

Two weeks after Clancy's death I found my way to the ocean to visit a friend's unused house on Fire Island. On Thursday Audrey had mentioned that her husband was going away that weekend. She had a car and suggested that we take Chico, one of the hospital cats, on a one-day excursion.

Chico was another cat who had been donated to the unit. His owners had brought him to the hospital when they noticed his open-mouthed breathing. He had a mass in his chest that was diagnosed as lymphosarcoma. Chico was unusual because he was leukemia test negative. (The majority of cats with lymphosarcoma in their chests are positive.) Frightened and aggressive at first, he was extremely difficult to handle. He was easily upset and sometimes created his own stress with a resulting shortness of breath. Treatments were not easy to administer, but with patience and minimal handling we found a system.

Chico actually belonged to the daughter in the family, and she had brought him in for treatment for nine months until she went away to school. Her parents did not want the responsibility of caring for him, and so she had asked us if we could help. We agreed to keep him.

Chico responded rapidly to therapy. With chemotherapy

the mass reduced 75 percent in size with his first treatment, and disappeared by the end of the first month.

Audrey drove out to catch the ferry to Fire Island on Friday night, and I picked up Chico from the hospital early Saturday morning on my way to the train. Audrey had left after work and expected a long drive in rush-hour traffic. We were afraid that Chico would become restless and overheated on such a drive. The train was air-conditioned, and he sat in the seat next to me with the front flap of the carrier open on the seat. I had a leash attached to his collar in case he tried to wander.

He seemed content sitting beside me and occasionally left his seat to join me in mine. When the conductor came by, Chico sat nicely in his carrier. I was always concerned when someone wanted to pet Chico because he nipped at fingers unexpectedly. He was being playful, and we who knew him had learned to hold still until he released us, but the natural impulse was to pull back the hand, and that encouraged Chico to tighten his grip. Fortunately the conductor simply nodded at us and walked on.

The ferry was a new experience for both of us. Chico turned his face to the wind, raising his chin slightly. The movement on the water didn't seem to bother him, and the openness of the ferry exposed us fully to the cool early morning air. The combination of a pre-season outing and the forecast of rain left us with an almost empty ferry.

When we reached land, I followed directions to a typical summer beach colony house, looking very much like the others on the dirt road. I saw Audrey sitting on the sun deck that covered half the second floor.

Chico and I explored the house as Audrey pointed out specific rooms. The bedrooms were small, with only a bed and dresser in each. The living room was light and airy with screened windows on three sides. Chico immediately settled in this main room, eying a vase of dried flowers and leaves. The kitchen had not yet been stocked with supplies, so we walked back into town to buy some coffee for us and some food for our companion.

When we got back, the sun came out briefly for Chico's benefit. We walked on the front lawn. We walked and Chico alternately pulled back on the leash, refusing to budge, and bounded on ahead of us, trying to free himself. We had planned to walk down to see the beach, but forty-five minutes later, when it started to rain, we had gotten only as far as the house next door.

Chico insisted upon sniffing each blade of grass, occasionally sampling one before his next cautious step. When the first drops of rain fell, he had discovered a weed and was methodically examining each leafy protrusion. It rained the entire day, and Chico slept in the living room while we read. He slept until he became bored. He chewed the dried branches, finally overturning the vase. We played with him for a while, and then I left the two of them and ventured out in the rain to the beach.

The waves were rough, slashing the beach with powerful gushing sounds. The ocean seemed angry, but the rain felt soft and sympathetic to my walk. As I wandered down the beach the sky grew darker and the day's mood changed. The rain fell more persistently, its coldness causing me to shiver. Thunder sounded in the distance. The waves slapped furiously and the thunder crept closer. When lightning flashed across the sky, it seemed as though the elements were competing. The waves thrashed against the shore as the sky growled and roared, electrified with light. Simultaneously frightened and exhilarated, I returned to the house.

We went into town for dinner, assuring Chico of a kitty bag. Chico slept in Audrey's room, and in the morning we left early to catch the returning ferry.

The horn sounded as the ferry pulled out and chugged from Fire Island to the mainland. Chico sat erect and felt the moisture in the air. His ears back, he waited fearlessly for something to happen. Audrey and I sat on either side of him, sensing his pleasure.

"He hates his leash," she commented.

"What kind of cat is that?" asked a passenger sitting behind us.

"He's part Abyssinian," Audrey replied, "and part unknown."

She was proud of Chico. He resembled a small mountain lion. He wore his black leather collar well.

Jay and Audrey shared custody of Chico, each taking him on alternate weekends. He was a community cat. We all shared the responsibility for his treatments, and the happiness of his well-being. Loving him was easy and rewarding, and for me it was a different kind of relationship than I had had with Clancy. Clancy had been mine, and his death had stunned me, filling my days with emptiness. I loved Chico, but I felt safer knowing that others loved him too.

It took three of us to treat him, and we only got one chance.

"He sounds like a fire engine," I commented as Jay gave him his injection the Friday after our trip.

"Where's the fire, Chico?" Audrey teased.

"He says it's in his eyes," I replied, moving my hand

quickly. Chico had been declawed on his front paws, but his teeth were large and formidable weapons. "Don't bite the nice nurse, Chico," I requested.

He sat up and snorted, then sprang from the table into the office.

"I'll see you around six, Chico," Jay reminded him, heading back to surgery. It was his turn to take him home this weekend.

"Don't forget, Jay. You know what happened last time."

We had left Chico's carrier open in the office so that he would know that he was going away that night. Jay didn't finish surgery until nine, and completely forgot about him. When we arrived the next morning, Chico had shredded the papers on Jay's desk and then used them as his litter box.

That rainy day at Fire Island was my only holiday escape that summer. I understood why New Yorkers flee the city on summer weekends. Summer was my least favorite season in New York. The cats and I were at a constant energy low. On humid days I left the air-conditioner on in the apartment when I went to work. Frederick enjoyed washing his front paws in the water bowl, usually before jumping on my lap, so I left extra bowls of fresh water for the others. We accepted summer as a long transition between spring and fall.

I missed the summers of my past, the summers that were never long enough. I missed the freedom of walking on the grass, of tripping along a winding dirt path broken by gnarled, protruding tree roots, down to the shore of a still unspoiled lake. Such excursions now mean checking train schedules or riding three hours to my destination.

I curbed my spontaneity when the cats became a part of my life. If I went away for more than one day I had to make arrangements for someone to feed them and change the litter.

Linda, one of the nurses at the AMC, was my first choice. In addition to meeting their basic needs she spent some time with them. Our ophthalmologist was an equally agreeable choice for the cats, and I returned the favor with her two cats when she went away. It wasn't the responsibility alone that limited my excursions. I missed them, and while it was possible to travel with one cat, it was impossible to choose only one of my five. Taking them all to an unfamiliar place was not a viable alternative.

So we spent the summer awaiting its end. My memories of past summers grew into dreams of the future. But my plans depended upon their being a part of that dream.

Chapter 8

In late July my mother called from Buffalo. She was crying.

"Dad's in the hospital," she began, "and this time I think it's bad."

Three years ago he had been hospitalized for surgery on his hip. The surgery had been postponed when the doctors discovered a suspicious area in his lungs on the X rays. They described their discovery to Mom as a "shadow" on Dad's lungs. They had not used the word *cancer*. When they sent him home after a few more weeks he seemed fine. Mom and Dad had said nothing to my brother and me about the X rays.

During the next three years Dad had been hospitalized several times. The doctors felt that he was strong enough to undergo two surgical procedures on his hip. Subsequently he had used a walker and had fallen a few times.

"What happened, Mom?" I asked.

"He had an attack, like a seizure. And when they took him to the hospital, they said that he has a brain tumor. He wants to see you, dear. He keeps asking for you and Paul."

My brother was married and lived in Wisconsin.

"Do you want me to call Paul?"

"I already did. He said he'll be here tomorrow. Can you come?"

Of course I could.

My father had cancer—a disease I hadn't even thought about before I started working at the center. Since then I had thought about it frequently, but mostly in terms of our patients. I subscribed to several medical journals, both human and veterinary, but even my reading was focused on the treatment of animals. I had heard of cases of my friends' friends or their relatives, but until now cancer had not touched my family directly.

He lay motionless in the hospital bed. Like a doll, he was manipulated into a different position and remained still until someone changed it. I reached for his bony hand and watched the protruding veins. Mom and Paul spoke to one another, occasionally posing a question to the ghostly figure who had brought us all together again. He responded with a grimace, a frown, and sometimes with a voice so fragile it might break. The doctors were busy, the nurses efficient, and he lay helpless on his bed and told us in such a way that he could not endure . . . the pain, the indignity, the loneliness— why could he not die? And we waited, all four, for the time.

We were a close family in many ways, but not an expressive one. Mom was fighting to maintain her self-control, that control that enabled her to work, visit Dad at the hospital, and think about the future, the near future. Paul and I were concerned that the emotions she was holding back would soon overwhelm her. But she had learned from her parents, as we had from ours, the private, individual depth of grief. Our conversations about Mom also served to distract us from that special sorrow that we both felt. We helped Mom by being there, by holding her hand or smiling across the room. We helped her and ourselves by loving her.

After a few days Paul and I returned to our jobs, leaving Mom alone to carry out the vigil. We were all waiting, but for Mom it was the hardest. Every day she witnessed the changes that time was making, changes that destroyed the stability of happier days.

My brother and I both needed to become totally involved in work. I spent long days at the clinic. Hours would pass when I would not think of Dad. I could think of death, I could focus on death as a concept, but I could not think of his death. To think of him was to relive his pain, a mental and physical anguish that I could do nothing to ease. We survivors, we who are left behind, know the frustration of helplessness. We carry on because it does not help if we don't. We function, not out of strength, but in the absence of any alternative. It was only at night, in the sanctuary of my home, that I could sit stroking Siggie, and feel the sorrow in my life.

Dad had shared his joy in music with Paul and me. Sitting in my living room, years from my childhood, hundreds of miles from my first home, with all the distance of life between us, I would listen to the music that he had made a part of my life. I could listen to Mozart or Wagner and think of nothing, clear my mind of any image, any thought. Once that moment was gone, I could cry. Because the music touched something within me, something that my mind would call sorrow—

sorrow at his inability to hear and to share this with me, sorrow for my own finite life, or anguish that the spirit can attain such heights while the body endures such pain. I could cry because things could not be as they were, because things would never again be the same.

Through the early days of August practical Siggie sent me off to work to earn his cat-food money. Linda and I joked about his voracious appetite. His three favorite things were food, Frederick, and me. Frederick and I could haggle for second place in Siggie's heart, but first place was decided by Siggie's stomach.

Natasha was appalled by Siggie's appetite. When I fed them together, Siggie devoured his dinner and then turned to the nearest plate for seconds. Natasha preferred to eat at a distance from Siggie, since she enjoyed a nice, leisurely meal.

I was prepared to share my dinner with the cats if I was brave enough to bring home fish. But one night I left a dish of steamed vegetables on the table when I left the room to answer the telephone. When I returned to the kitchen, I discovered Sam eating my cauliflower and Daphne manipulating an ear of corn with one paw while gnawing at the kernels. They saved the broccoli for me.

Natasha and Siggie responded to my needs, seizing every opportunity to sit with me. Frederick danced on my lap, honoring me by cleaning my arm with his sandpaper tongue. When I could tolerate the ritual no more and displaced him, he sought out Sam for a tumble. Daphne had her own needs. If she wasn't receiving enough attention from me, she threw herself at my occasional guests, running out with them into the hall when they left.

A Monday morning in August my mother called. She had

gone to the hospital earlier than usual that morning, and Dad had waited for her arrival. As she reached his bed he sought her hand, and with his weary, pain-laden eyes he gazed at her. His love for her had begun over thirty years ago, and he could not leave without once more seeing her. But the pain this last time was more real than his desire to stay with her. Death offered him relief, and he accepted.

As Mom and I entered the room I paused to read the notes attached to the floral arrangements, lamenting the fate of these lovely flowers, clipped and solemnly arranged to represent years of friendship and now sorrow. Their burden was heavy.

He lay in his Sunday suit, the navy blue, with an unfashionably narrow striped tie.

"He never liked his Bloomingdale's ties, did he?" I smiled at Mom.

"He loved them, dear. That's why he kept them in his drawer. He used to like looking at them."

I couldn't remember when I first deliberately chose to love him. I had been his favorite in many ways, perhaps because he saw himself in me. I was quiet and independent as he was, especially before he met Mom. We were both stubborn and proud. He had always supported my whims. He shared his love for music, art, and antiques with me. And he loved animals.

"Poor Mitchie," I said, "I'll bet he misses Dad. Who'll buy him chicken livers now?"

"And who else would open five different cans of cat food until Mitchie finds one he likes?" Mom asked.

"You probably would," I replied.

The paste-white face was handsome, but austere and loveless. I turned away. Friends appeared, and the room grew lively with conversation. The reunion let me momentarily forget the occasion. Sometimes my eyes would drift back to the casket, and someone, following my glance, would remark how nice he looked. In a gesture of comfort others would speak of his suffering and the relief that followed its termination. Before me flashed the image of my father in his hospital room, eaten away by disease and reminded only by pain and sorrow of the life still in him. A team united in purpose strove to keep him alive, while those who loved him prayed that he would die.

The burial took place on a gloomy Friday morning. It was windy and cold in the openness of the cemetery, the kind of day that Dad had always hated. Mom, Paul, and I waited in the gray drizzle, our feet sinking into the soggy earth. The station wagon arrived, and the men gathered to lift the heavy urn that contained his ashes. It fell to the ground. Mom shuddered and turned away. When they had lowered it into the ground and returned the first pieces of moist earth to their place, we joined hands, the three of us, and said good-bye. The sun, previously hidden by a thick pattern of clouds, broke through for just a moment in our final farewell.

I returned to New York the next afternoon. Siggie sat on the floor, gazing soulfully at me with his golden eyes, waiting for encouragement to come up and sit with me. Daphne was not so respectful. Having known me longer, she knew that she could make her usual demands. Sam and Frederick fought, and Sam wore the evidence of defeat on his tail. Natasha went to the laundry bag, selected a dirty sock, and, meowing as she dragged it through the apartment, deposited it selflessly at my feet. How good life was—full of kindness and instinct, love and dirty socks.

I had two days before returning to work. I had two days to feel intensely, to remember lovingly. Two days to share the things that he had loved, and then to let go. The love would remain, expressing itself daily in the living beings who shared my life. Once I returned to work, the habits and demands of my daily life would dominate. There would be no shared memories, for no one here knew him. No one here noticed that he was gone.

In September I registered at Hunter College for a microbiology course. I had graduated from Hunter with a major in English and had continued my studies in graduate school. When I started working in oncology as a research associate, I found my interest drawn to the sciences. My mother reminded me that as a child I worked on my brother's science projects. She interpreted my enthusiasm retrospectively as an early inclination for the field. I think that I enjoyed the challenge of solving a problem, but even more, I think that I wanted to please my big brother.

In school I had avoided elective science courses. It was not until I had worked at the center for two or three years that I recognized my need for and developing interest in science.

I had become familiar with the drugs and dosages, learning for which diseases particular drugs were most effective. I could recognize symptoms and anticipate problems in treatment. When the oncology service did its hospital rounds, I was included. I listened as they discussed each case. I learned what they suspected from the clinical history and symptoms, which tests they requested to establish a diagnosis, and what the diagnosis meant in terms of the animal's life. And then I read about each disease, possible treatments, complications due to treatment. I read about similar diseases and therapy in humans. I subscribed to medical and oncology journals. I read with an understanding based solely on my still limited clinical experience.

But I had reached a point in my scientific career where I needed basic background information. I was trying to master advanced concepts without having learned the fundamentals. So I decided to return to undergraduate study at night. I had no particular goal in mind, except to learn as much as possible about my new field. Each semester I enrolled in one of the courses that I had avoided in my previous academic career. I began with biology.

The microbiology course that I registered for now met once a week on Monday, my day off. It involved a two-hour lecture with a three-hour lab. I enjoyed studying and especially looked forward to the weekly lab.

Lab was my opportunity to understand what I had studied and memorized in lecture. I wanted to learn so that I could apply this knowledge to my work. I could study for exams, I could perfect my laboratory technique, but the true value of my studying became apparent when I understood something at work because of my efforts. When I read an article and it referred to some test that I had performed in lab, I felt that I was making progress.

Chapter 9

With work and school the fall weeks passed quickly. In late October I somehow exposed my cats to an upper respiratory tract virus. Natasha, Daphne, and Siggie remained healthy, but Sam and Frederick became quite ill. Upper respiratory infections (URI) are highly contagious among cats. They are airborne viruses and do not depend upon direct cat-to-cat contact. Even though I was careful about washing my hands after handling a sick cat, I probably brought the virus home on my clothes.

Sneezing, runny noses, red, weepy eyes. Frederick's nose was so congested that he had to breathe through his mouth. They couldn't smell food and wouldn't eat on their own. I didn't want to expose the ward cats, so I kept the two boys, who finally had something in common, home. Sam responded quickly to treatment and soon began to eat on his own. Frederick had a more severe case. He felt miserable, but he was a wonderful patient. I fed him, gave him fluids to prevent dehydration, ointment for his eyes, and antibiotics in case of a secondary bacterial infection. For days we fought to keep him stable, to prevent him from getting weaker. It was a joyous day when he licked baby food off my finger. We had reached the turning point. I went to work feeling optimistic for the first time in two weeks.

Clinic started early, and I had little time to think about my private patient. I felt almost light-headed from lack of worry.

When I walked into the office, Audrey was talking about a new patient.

"She wants to euthanize him, but it's her husband's cat, and he's away on business."

"Who's that, Audrey?" I asked.

"The cat's name is Rasputin. I told her we'd try to help him while she gets in touch with the husband, but the cat's really in bad shape. Wait till you see him."

"Leukemia test positive?" I asked.

"Yes, and pale as a ghost. I think we'll put him in a cage, and I'd like you to put in a catheter for his blood transfusion, if you don't mind. I'll help hold him."

"Do you think he can wait until you're free?"

"Well, he's waited this long, and I don't want him struggling with anyone else."

I carried the young black and white cat to his cage. He cried as though in pain, but he was so weak that he couldn't move. I called Audrey and asked her if I could give him an intravenous drug used for treatment of shock while he waited for his blood. She agreed that it might make him feel better. He let me insert the needle without a struggle, and remained quiet while I gave the drug slowly. I thought he was going to die any moment.

As soon as Audrey was free, I inserted the catheter into his jugular vein and we took our blood samples for the lab. He was lying still in his cage when she left, receiving the blood transfusion. I sat next to him and put my finger on the whitened pads of his right front paw. His nails curled around my finger. I wanted him to know that someone was there. As he lay there he urinated on the cardboard pad, and didn't have the strength to move from that spot. I lifted him and changed the pad. When I left, he still had not moved.

"Well, at least we've done all that we can," I remarked to Audrey on our way out of the building.

"Now it's up to him," she replied. "Did he seem more comfortable?"

"He stopped that plaintive meowing, so he may feel better."

Thursday afternoon, two days after he arrived, I read a notation in Rasputin's record that he was depressed. When I opened the cage door, however, to sit with him, he immediately came and sat on my lap.

"Well, Rasputin, have you figured out what happened to that one day in your life? I think you lost it, and we almost lost you."

He was purring and rolling, slipping off my lap and climbing back on. I was stroking his sparkling white tummy, and he was gazing at me with dreamy, faraway eyes. Siggie eyes, I call them.

"You didn't think life was so good that day, did you? And now look at you. The days just aren't long enough for all the catching up you want to do."

Finally he decided he was hungry again and climbed down from my lap to eat. I changed his litter pan and looked for Audrey.